CHESS FOR YOU

CHESS FOR YOU

THE EASY BOOK FOR BEGINNERS
BY ROBERT S. FENTON

A THISTLE BOOK

Published by
GROSSET & DUNLAP, INC.
A National General Company
New York

Copyright © 1973 Grosset & Dunlap, Inc.
All Rights Reserved
Published simultaneously in Canada

Library of Congress Catalog Card Number 72-94238
ISBN: 0-448-21476-8 (trade edition)
ISBN: 0-448-26240-1 (library edition)

Printed in the United States of America

To
My friend,
Phil L.

Contents

STARTING TO PLAY	1
1 The Beginning	3
2 How the Chessmen Move	6
3 Capturing	13
4 The Power of the Chessmen	22
5 Check and Checkmate	25
6 Castling	34
7 Start to Play	38
PLAYING TO WIN	43
8 Names and Abbreviations	45
9 The Opening	48
10 Early Queen Attacks	55
11 When and How to Attack	60
12 Planning to Win	64
13 More Openings	66
ADVANCED RULES AND SUGGESTIONS	69
14 More on Check	71
15 En Passant	74
16 Draws	76
17 Touch-Move	80
18 Final Thoughts	83

STARTING TO PLAY

CHAPTER 1

The Beginning

To play chess you need a chessboard, chessmen, and an opponent. (Your opponent is the person who plays the game against you.)

The Chessboard

A chessboard looks like a checkerboard, but when playing chess make sure that the white corner square is on your near right side. (You'll never forget this if you remember the saying, "white on the right.")

This is your opponent's side of
the board.

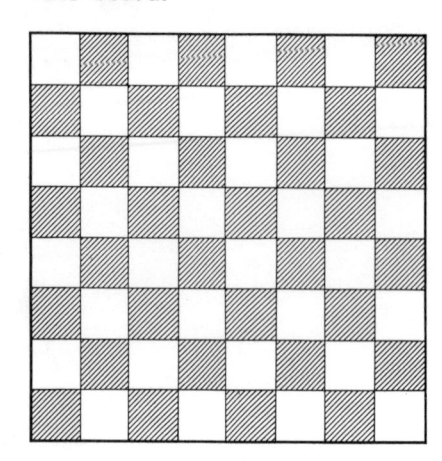

Diagram 1

white corner square

This is your side of the board.

Notice that the *other* white corner square is on your opponent's near right side. (Turn the diagram upside down and you'll see that that's true.)

The Chessmen

The chessmen in each chess set come in two colors. We always call the lighter color *White* and the darker color *Black*.

Diagram 2 shows the shapes of the chessmen.

King
(The
tallest
piece)

Queen
(Second
tallest
piece)

Rook
(Looks
like a
castle
tower)

Bishop
(Looks
like a
Bishop's
hat)

Knight
(Looks
like
horse's
head)

Pawn
(Smallest
chessman)

Diagram 2

4

At the start of a game each side has 16 chessmen, as shown in Diagram 3, below. In a chess book these small pictures are used to identify each of the pieces.

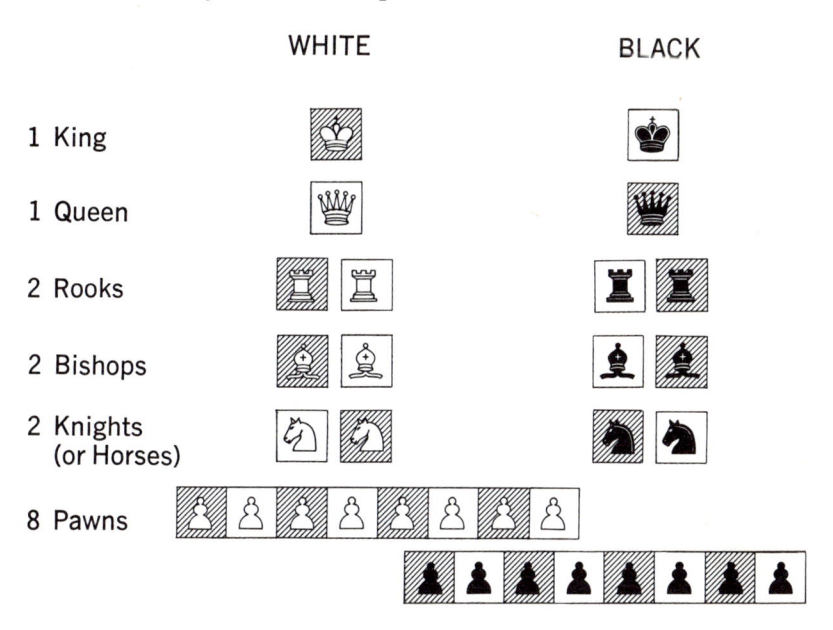

WHITE BLACK

1 King

1 Queen

2 Rooks

2 Bishops

2 Knights
(or Horses)

8 Pawns

Diagram 3

CHAPTER 2

How the Chessmen Move

How the KING moves

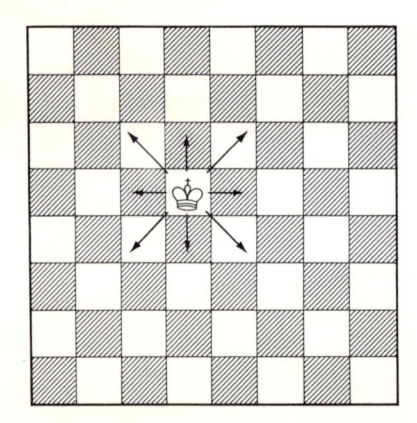

Diagram 4

The King is the tallest piece. He usually has a cross on the top of his crown.

The King moves *one* square in any direction. He may move one square:

> Forward,
> Backward,
> Sideways, or
> Diagonally (on a slant).

This sign may help you remember how the King moves: ✳

6

How the ROOK moves

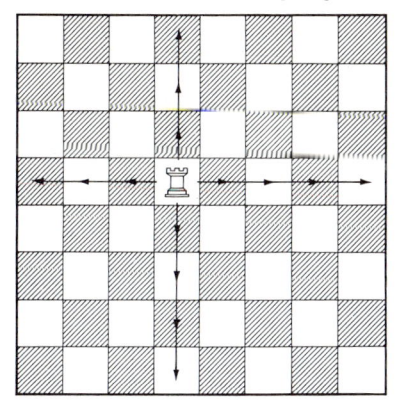

Diagram 5

The Rook looks like a castle-tower.

The Rook may move as many squares as it wants:

>Forward,
>Backward, or
>Sideways.

Put one of your own Rooks on the chessboard and practice moving him as Diagram 5 shows. Remember: The Rook may go as many squares in one direction as you wish to move him.

This sign may help you remember how the Rook moves: +

How the BISHOP moves

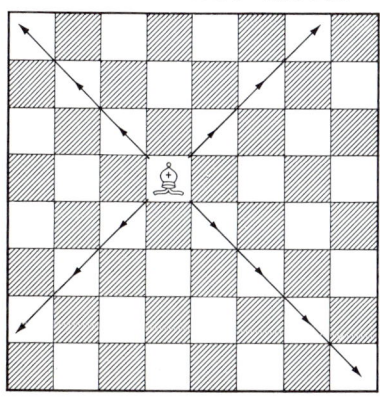

Diagram 6

This piece is shaped like the pointed hat worn by a Bishop.

The Bishop may move as many squares as he wants, diagonally (on a slant).

7

Move the Bishop on your own chessboard, just as Diagram 6 shows.

At the start of a game, each player has one Bishop on a white square and one Bishop on a black square. Since Bishops can move only diagonally, a Bishop which starts out on a white square will move on the white squares of the chessboard all through the game; and a Bishop which starts out on a black square will stay on the black squares all through the game.

A sign for how the Bishop moves might look like this: ✕

How the QUEEN moves

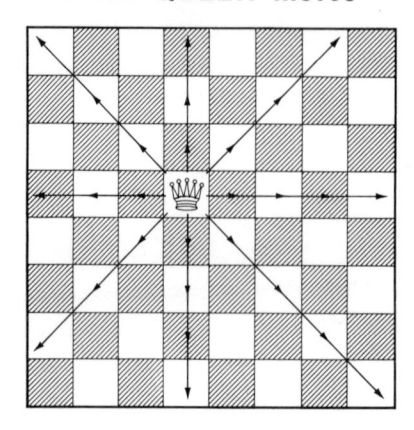

Diagram 7

The Queen is taller than any piece except the King.

The Queen is very strong. She combines the moving ability of a Rook and a Bishop. She may move as many squares as she wants:

> Forward,
> Backward,
> Sideways, or
> Diagonally (on a slant).

On your own chessboard practice moving the Queen as Diagram 7 shows.

A sign for how the Queen moves might look like this: ✶

Note on the Rook, Bishop, and Queen:

On any single move each of these pieces may go in one direction only. As an example, the Rook may not move two squares forward and three squares sideways *as part of one move.* He may, however, move two squares forward on one move, and then he may move three squares sideways on his *next* move.

How the KNIGHT moves

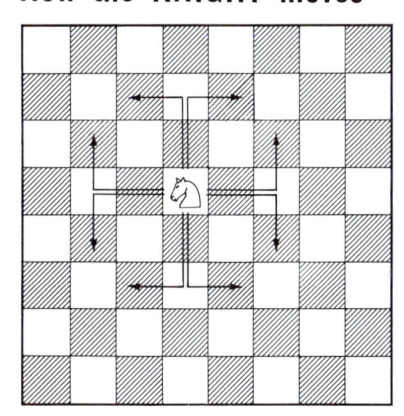

Diagram 8

Knights rode on horses, so the Knight in chess is shaped like a horse's head.

The Knight moves "two out and one over."

Put one of your Knights on the chessboard and move him just as Diagram 8 shows. Be sure to count the squares carefully as you say to yourself, "Two out and one over."

The Knight is not allowed to move just one square and then stop, or to move two squares and then stop. When he moves he *must* move "two out and one over."

The Knight is a very tricky character. He is the only chessman who can *leap over* pieces.

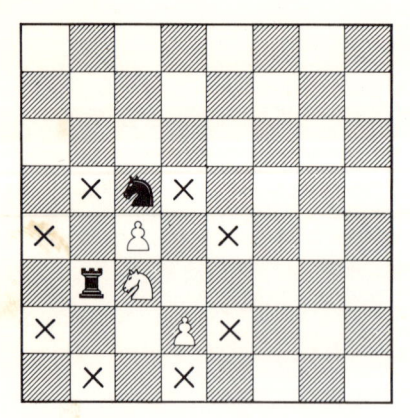

Diagram 9

In Diagram 9 the White Knight can move to any of the squares marked with an X—just as if none of the other chessmen were on the board! An abbreviation for how the Knight moves might look like this: ⊢┼┤

How the PAWN moves

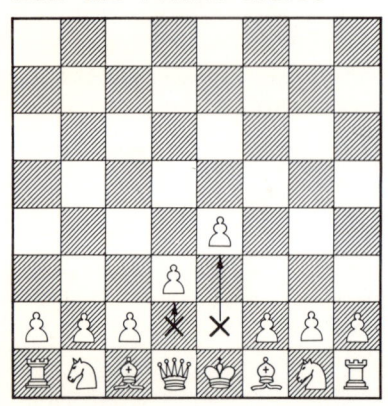

Diagram 10

The Pawn is the smallest of the chessmen.

The Pawn moves straight forward.

On its *first* move each Pawn has a choice: it may go one square forward or two squares forward. In Diagram 10 one of the Pawns went two squares forward on its first move. The Pawn to its left moved only one square forward on its first move. These two Pawns may move only one square at a time from now on.

The Pawn moves differently when it is capturing one of the opponent's pieces. This is explained in the next chapter.

Sometimes a Pawn can change into a Queen Compared to the other chessmen, a Pawn moves very slowly; but if a Pawn gets all the way to the opposite end of the board it changes into a powerful Queen!

Here's how a Pawn turns into a Queen:

BLACK	Black's side of the board	WHITE
1st Rank		8th Rank
2nd Rank	Y ♙	7th Rank
3rd Rank		6th Rank
4th Rank		5th Rank
5th Rank		4th Rank
6th Rank		3rd Rank
7th Rank	♟ X	2nd Rank
8th Rank		1st Rank

White's side of the board

Diagram 11

On a chessboard there are eight rows of squares that run across from side to side. These rows are called Ranks. *Your* first Rank is the row closest to you, your opponent's first Rank is the row closest to him. In Diagram 11 each Rank is numbered for both players.

In Diagram 11 the White Pawn started off in the square marked with an X. It has finally gone to a square on its 7th Rank. At the very moment it moves into a square on its 8th Rank, it changes into a White Queen.

The same thing is true for the Black Pawn. It started off in the square marked with a Y, and is now in a square on its 7th Rank. As soon as it moves into a square on its 8th Rank, it changes into a Black Queen.

When a Pawn has reached its 8th Rank, take it off the board

and put a new Queen in its place. Each Pawn that is pushed forward to its 8th Rank is promoted into another Queen. (If your chess set doesn't have extra Queens for this purpose, use spools of white or black thread, or salt or pepper shakers, or some other objects, to stand for the extra Queens.)

Actually, a Pawn which reaches the other side of the board *may* be changed into a Rook or Bishop or Knight; but since a Queen is more powerful than these pieces, you'd almost always choose to change your Pawn into another Queen. (However, a Pawn may never be changed into a King.)

The Pawn is the only chessman which can ever be changed into another piece. *No other piece, no matter what square on the chessboard it reaches, can be changed into anything else.*

SUMMARY

The KING moves one square in any direction. ✳

The ROOK moves any number of squares forward, backward, or sideways. ┼

The BISHOP moves any number of squares diagonally. ✕

The QUEEN moves any number of squares forward, backward, sideways, or diagonally. ✳

The KNIGHT moves "two out and one over." ┤┼┤

The PAWN, on its first move, moves straight forward one or two squares, but from then on it may move only one square at a time. The Pawn can never move backward or sideways. ↑

Whenever a Pawn reaches the other end of the board (its 8th Rank) it is immediately promoted into a Queen.

CHAPTER 3

Capturing

One of the most important things you can do is to capture your opponent's chessmen. In this way you can weaken him so that he'll have less power with which to attack your King and less power with which to defend his own King.

You capture an enemy piece by landing on it; that is, by moving one of your pieces onto a square occupied by one of your opponent's men. You then take the opponent's chessman off the board. You have "taken" him or "captured" him, and he is out of the game.

You don't *have* to capture a piece just because you're able to; you may make some other move instead.

No piece may make more than one capture on any single move.

Of course, you are never allowed to capture any of your own chessmen.

Capturing with the KING ✳

Diagram 12

In Diagram 12 the White King may capture either Black's Pawn or Knight.

PUZZLES

Diagram 12-A

Question: Can the White King capture the Black Rook?

Answer: He can capture the Rook or the Knight—whichever he chooses.

Diagram 12-B

Question: Can the White King capture the Black Queen?

Answer: The King may move only one square in any direction. Therefore he cannot capture the Queen. (However, he can capture the Pawn.)

Capturing with the ROOK

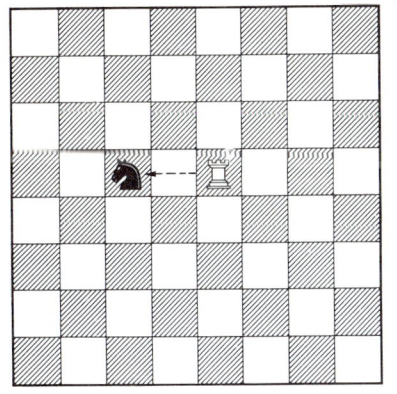

Diagram 13

In Diagram 13 it's White's move. His Rook may capture Black's Knight, as the arrow shows.

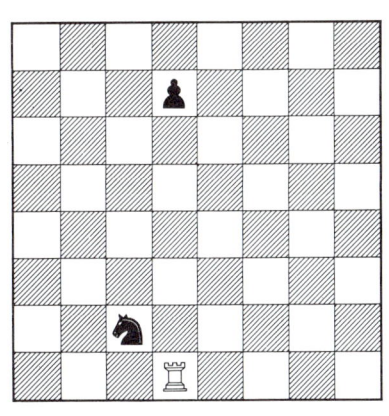

PUZZLES

Diagram 13-A

Question: The White Rook may capture the Pawn. Can he capture the Knight?

Answer: Since the Rook cannot move diagonally, he cannot capture the Knight.

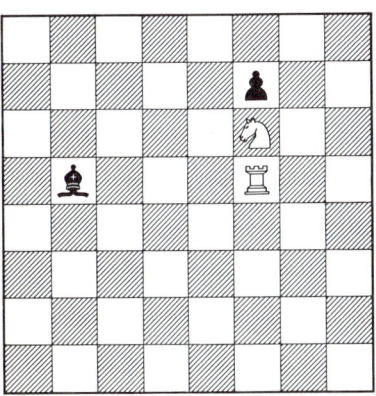

Diagram 13-B

Question: The White Rook may capture the Bishop. Can he capture the Pawn?

Answer: The Rook cannot capture the Pawn until he first moves his own Knight out of the way.

Capturing with the BISHOP ✕

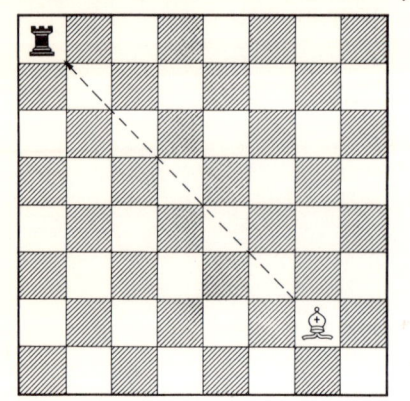

Diagram 14

The White Bishop may capture the Black Rook, as the arrow shows.

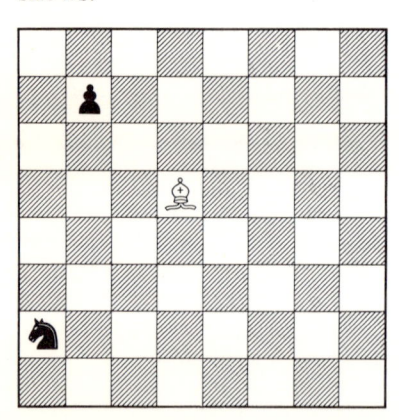

PUZZLES

Diagram 14-A

Question: Can White's Bishop capture the Black Pawn? Can he capture the Black Knight?

Answer: The Bishop is attacking both of Black's chessmen. He can capture whichever one he chooses to.

Diagram 14-B

Question: Which of Black's men can the Bishop capture on this move?

Answer: Only the Pawn on the black square.

Capturing with the QUEEN

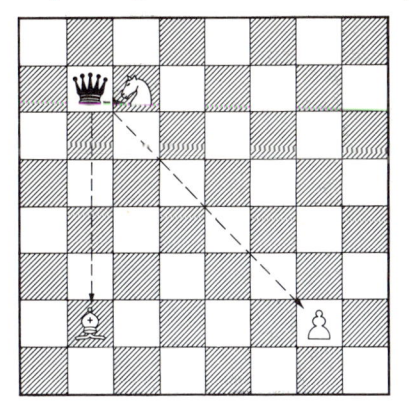

Diagram 15

This time it's Black's move. His Queen can capture the Knight, or the Pawn, or the Bishop!

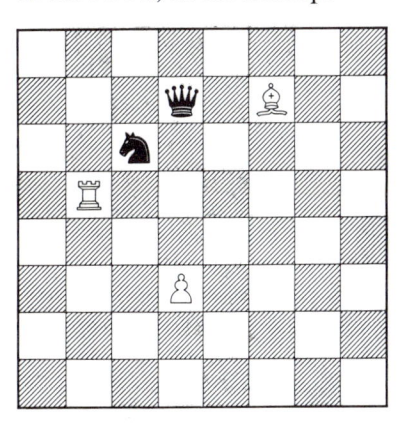

PUZZLES

Diagram 15-A

Question: Which of White's men can the Black Queen capture?

Answer: The Black Queen can capture either the Bishop or the Pawn, but cannot capture the Rook until the Black Knight gets out of the way.

Diagram 15-B

Question:
(1) Which of White's men can the Black Queen capture?
(2) If it were White's turn to move, which of his pieces could capture the Black Queen?

Answer:
(1) She can capture any one of White's eight pieces!
(2) If it were White's move, only the Bishop on the black square could capture the Queen.

Capturing with the KNIGHT

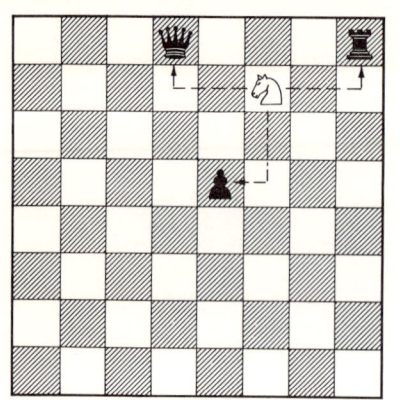

"Two out and one over"

Diagram 16

Diagram 16 shows how tricky the Knight is. He can capture Black's Queen, Rook, or Pawn, as he chooses.

PUZZLES

Diagram 16-A

Question: Which of Black's pieces can the White Knight capture?

Answer: Either the Bishop or the Rook. (The Knight can skip over pieces but captures only the piece which is standing on the square where the Knight's move comes to an end.)

Diagram 16-B

Question: The White Knight can capture only one of Black's men. Which one?

Answer: The Bishop standing on the black square. Remember that a Knight moves "two out and one over."

Capturing with the PAWN

As you know, the Pawn moves straight ahead—but it *captures* in a different way. This sign may help you remember how the Pawn moves when capturing: ↖↗

Diagram 17

In Diagram 17 the White Pawn can capture Black's Pawn or Black's Queen, but it may not capture the Black Knight (and it cannot move straight ahead until the Black Knight gets out of the way).

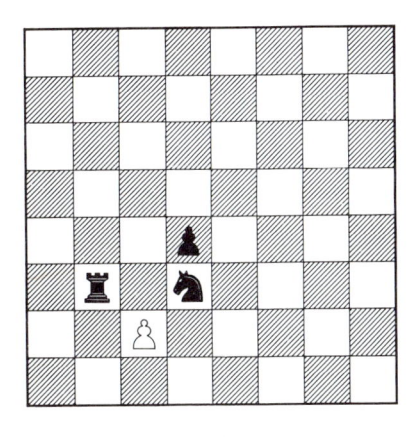

PUZZLE

Diagram 17-A

Question: White's Pawn is going to make its first move. What are the four different moves it can make?

Answer: White's Pawn may:
(1) Capture the Black Rook,
(2) Capture the Black Knight,
(3) Move one square straight forward, or
(4) Move two squares straight forward.

19

CAPTURING PUZZLES

In Diagrams X, Y, and Z it is White's turn to move. In each case he may capture enemy pieces if he chooses to do so.

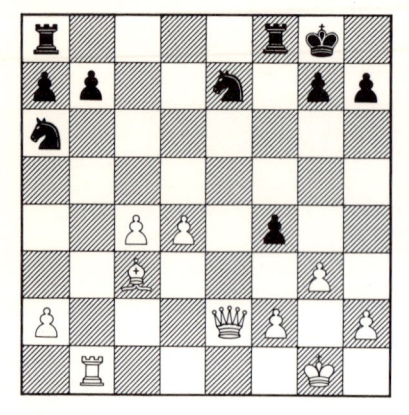

Diagram X

Question: What chessmen may White capture?

Answer: White's Rook is threatening a black Pawn; White's Queen is attacking a Black Knight; a white Pawn is attacking a Black Pawn. White may make any one of these captures.

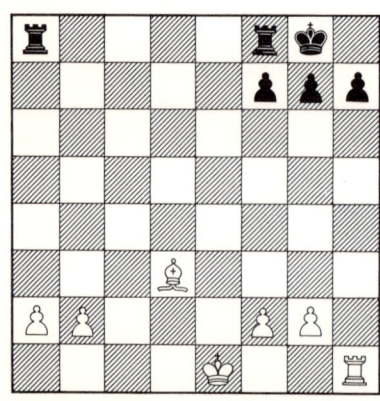

Diagram Y

Question: What captures may White make?

Answer: White's Bishop and Rook are both attacking the same Black Pawn. (It's a good idea to threaten one particular square with two or more of your own men.)

Diagram Z

Question: Here's a very powerful attack by White on a Black Pawn. Which White pieces are threatening the Pawn?

Answer: In this example, three White pieces are attacking the same Black Pawn. They are White's Knight, Bishop, and Rook. (The Knight is also attacking another Black Pawn.)

SUMMARY

One of the most important things in chess is to weaken your opponent by capturing his pieces. Before each of your moves, look over the board to see if you can take any of his men. If you can't, then it may be wise to make a move now which threatens to capture one of his pieces on your next turn.

Copy the following signs on a sheet of paper and keep it by your chessboard to help you remember how the chessmen move:

King ✳

Queen ✳

Rook +

Bishop ✕

Knight "Two out and one over" ⊢⊣

Pawn ↑ ↖↗
     (move) (capture)

Diagram 18

CHAPTER 4

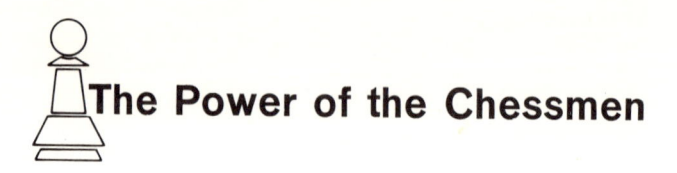

The Power of the Chessmen

Some of your chessmen are more important to you than others because they have more power. The diagram below shows you about how important each chessman is. (The numbers in the diagrams are not for keeping score. They are used only to help you remember which pieces are "bigger" than others.)

Each PAWN has a value of 1.
Each KNIGHT has a value of 3.
Each BISHOP has a value of 3.
Each ROOK has a value of 5.
Each QUEEN has a value of 9.

Diagram 19

You may be wondering why the King is not included in Diagram 19. The reason is that he has a special importance—for if *he* is lost, the *game* is lost!

The main idea for you to keep in mind is to try to win your opponent's more important pieces while losing only smaller pieces of your own.

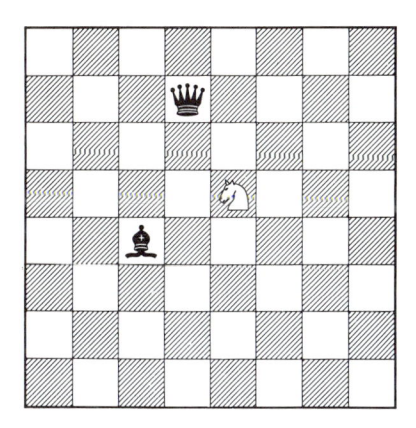

PUZZLE

Diagram 20

Question: The White Knight can capture either the Bishop or the Queen. Which one should he take?

Answer: The Queen, because she has a value of 9. She is more important than the Bishop (a value of 3).

During your games, if you have a choice, capture your opponent's bigger piece.

Exchanges

Sometimes in your games you'll be able to take one of your opponent's men without losing any pieces of your own. But very often if you capture one of his pieces he will then take one of yours. This is called an "exchange."

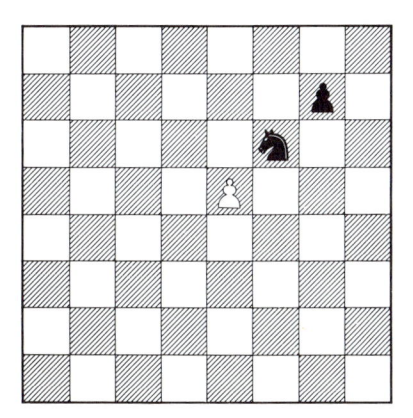

Diagram 21

It's White's turn to move. If his Pawn captures the Black Knight, then Black's Pawn takes the White Pawn. White would win a Knight (a value of 3) and lose a Pawn (a value of 1). It would be a good exchange for him. (This is called "winning the exchange.")

23

Diagram 22

If White's Rook captures the Black Bishop, then the Black Knight (which is protecting his Bishop), captures White's Rook. White would win a Bishop (a value of 3) but lose a Rook (a value of 5). It would *not* be a good exchange for White. (This is called "losing the exchange.)

PUZZLE

Diagram 23

Question: If White captured Black's Queen he would then lose his Rook. Should White make that move?

Answer: Yes, because he would win a Queen (worth 9), which is more valuable than a Rook (worth 5).

CHAPTER 5

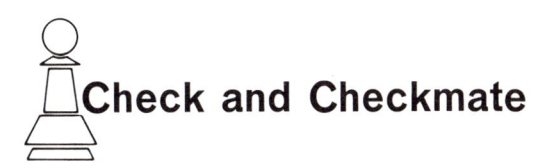

Check and Checkmate

"Check" means that a direct attack is being made on a King.

"Checkmate" means that a King is in Check and cannot escape. A game is won when a player Checkmates his opponent's King.

Now let's look at Check and Checkmate one at a time:

CHECK

In earlier diagrams you saw how a Pawn attacked (that is, threatened to capture) a Knight—or a Rook attacked a Bishop, and so on. Whenever a direct attack is made on a *King,* that King is said to be "in Check."

When a player puts his opponent's King in Check he says, out loud, "Check," which means: "I am now directly attacking your King."

25

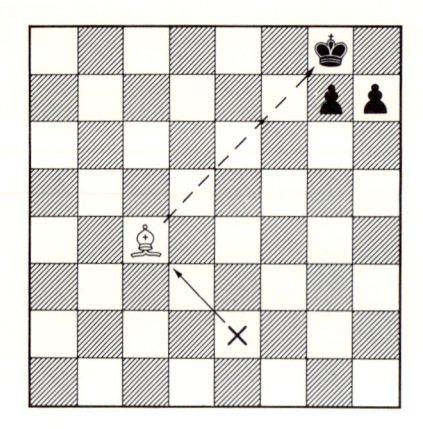

Diagram 24

White has just moved his Bishop from the square marked with an X to the position shown in the diagram. The Bishop is now directly attacking the Black King. The player with the White pieces says: "Check!" Now the King must try to escape.

More Examples of Check   In each of the next four diagrams White has just moved and Checked the Black King.

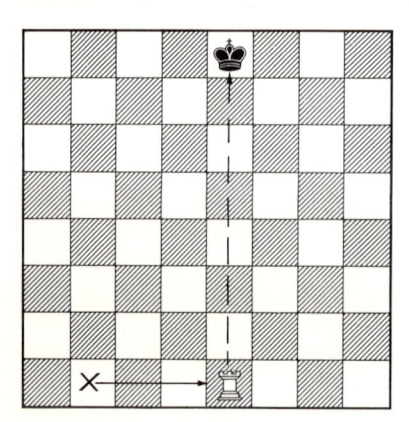

Diagram 25

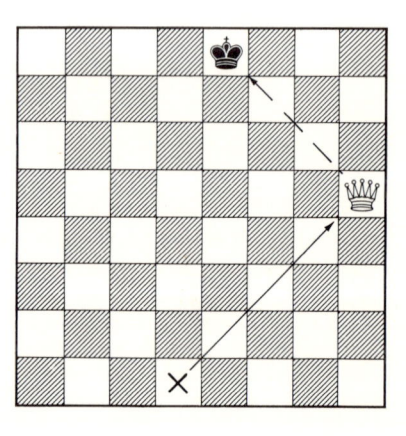

Diagram 26

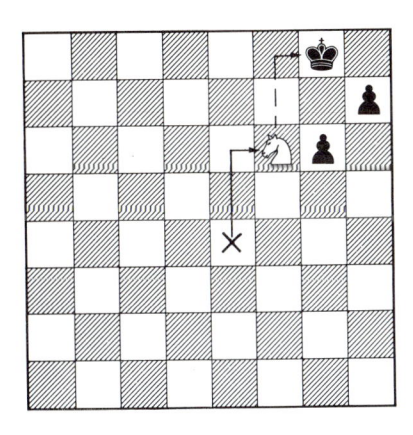

Diagram 27

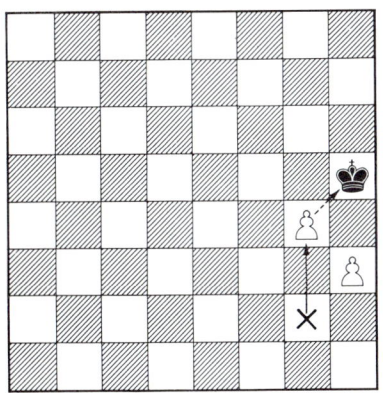

Diagram 28

What a Player Must Do When His King Is Checked   The rule is that he must stop the Check against his King *immediately*. He is never allowed to do *anything* else.

If he makes some other move by mistake, which leaves his King in Check, he *must* take that move back; it does not count.

If the player *can't* get his King out of Check, he is Checkmated and loses the game.

How to Get Out of Check   There are three different ways for a player to get his King out of Check:

1. By moving his King to a safe square (a square which is not attacked by any of his opponent's pieces);
2. By moving one of his men between his King and the attacking piece;
3. By capturing the piece which is Checking his King.

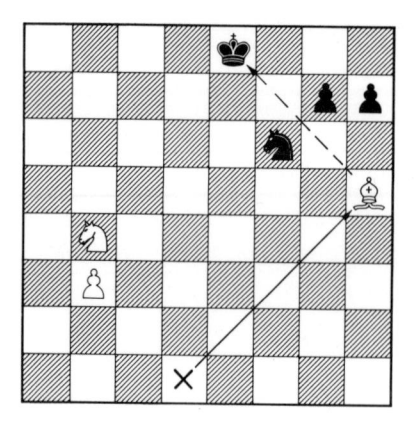

Diagram 29

In Diagram 29 White has just moved his Bishop and Checked the Black King. Now it's Black's move, and he must get out of Check. In this case, Black can do any one of the three things listed on page 27, as shown in the next three diagrams:

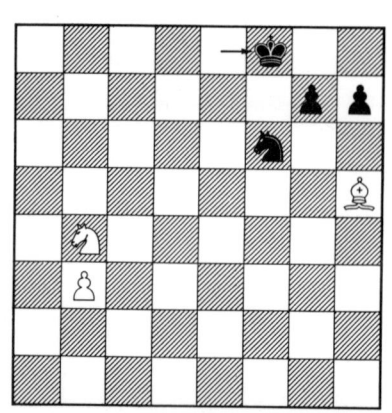

Diagram 30-A

The Black King has moved to a square that is not attacked by either White's Bishop or any other White piece. The King is now out of Check.

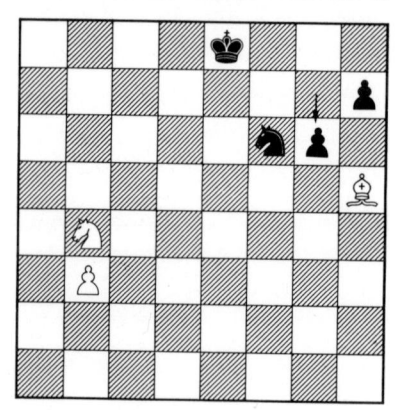

Diagram 30-B

Black has moved one of his men (a Pawn) between his King and White's attacking piece. His King is now out of Check.

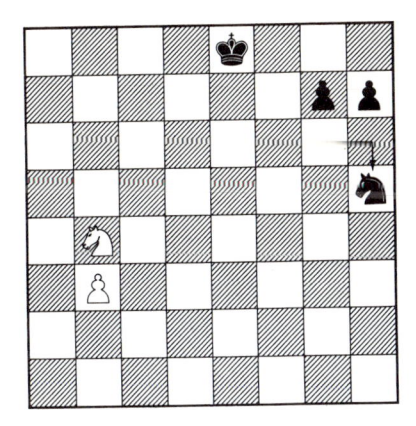

Diagram 30-C

In Diagram 30-C, Black's Knight has captured White's Bishop, and the Black King is no longer in Check.

If your King is Checked all of a sudden in the middle of a game, don't be too quick to grab him and move him to a safe square. *Before* you touch any of your pieces, ask yourself: "Can I capture the piece which is Checking me? Can I move one of my men between my King and the piece which is Checking me?" If you find more than one way to get out of Check, take your time to decide which way is best.

PUZZLES

In Diagram 31 the Black Knight has just Checked the White King. None of White's pieces can capture the Knight. The only way the White King can get out of Check is to move to one of three different safe squares.

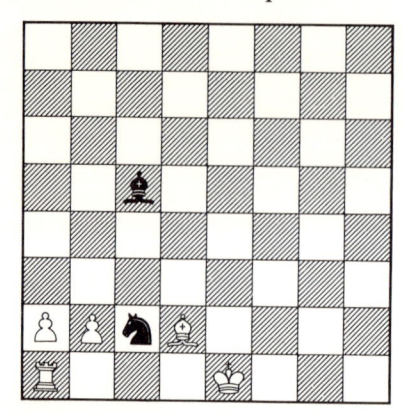

Diagram 31

Questions:
1. Can you find those three safe squares?
2. After the White King has moved to a safe square, what is the Knight's best move?

Answers:
1. The King may move sideways to the left, straight forward, or sideways to the right. (He cannot move diagonally to the upper right because that square is attacked by the Black Bishop.)
2. The Black Knight's best move would be to capture the White Rook.

In Diagram 32 the Black Bishop has Checked the White King.

Diagram 32

Question: What would be the white King's best move?

Answer: The White King may escape from Check by moving either sideways to the left or sideways to the right; but his best move would be to capture the Bishop.

Diagram 33 is the same as Diagram 32, except that now Black has a Rook protecting his Bishop.

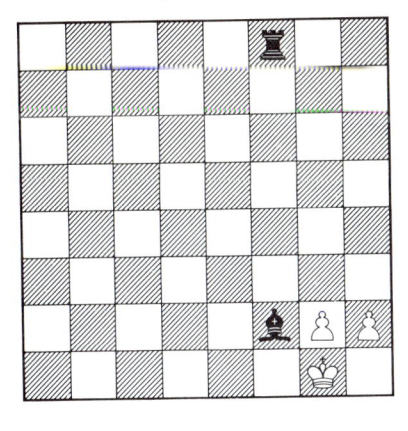

Diagram 33

Question: What can the White King do to escape from Check?

Answer: The King can get out of Check by moving sideways to his left or sideways to his right. White's King is not allowed to capture the Black Bishop in Diagram 33 because the King would then be moved into a square attacked by the Black Rook. (A King is never allowed to move into Check.)

CHECKMATE

If a King is Checked and cannot get out of Check, then he is "Checkmated." As soon as that happens, the game is over, and the winner is the player who has Checkmated his opponent's King.

The next six diagrams show some of the ways a player may Checkmate the enemy King. In each case the arrow shows how White moved to Check the Black King in such a way that the King couldn't escape.

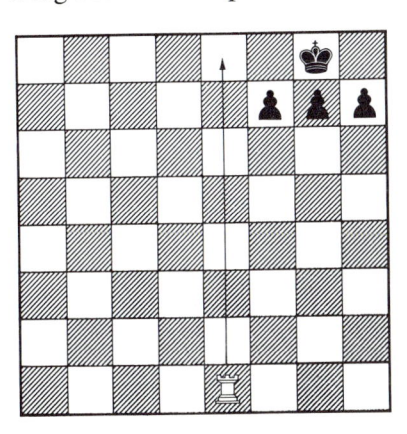

Diagram 34

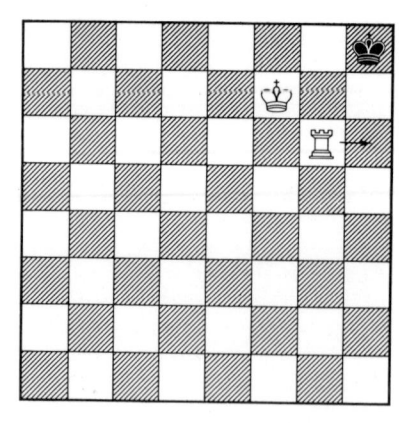

Diagram 35

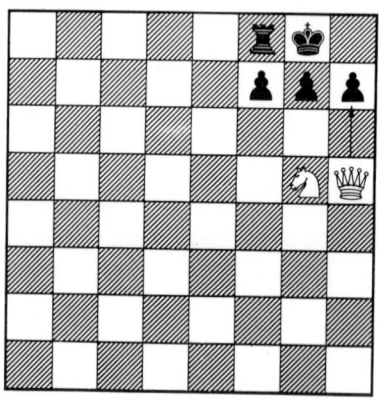

Diagram 36

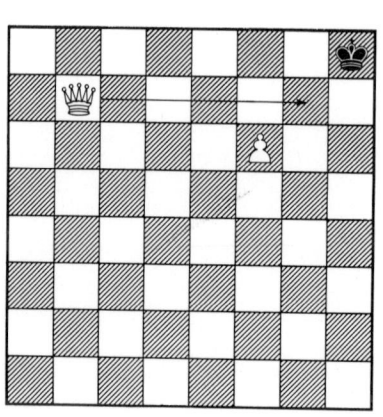

Diagram 37

32

Diagram 38

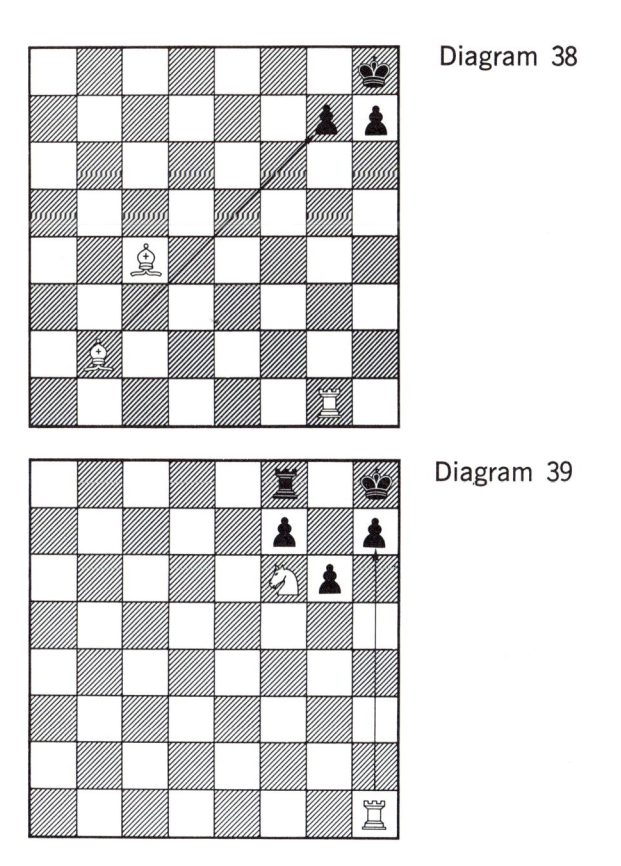

Diagram 39

Set up your own chessboard as shown in the diagrams, and make the move that wins for White. Try to understand clearly why it is Checkmate in each example.

33

CHAPTER 6

Castling

"Castling" is the name of an extremely important move. In Castling, a player moves both his King and his Rook *at the same time* in a special manner.

Castling helps a player in two ways:

1. He tucks his King safely behind his own Pawns; and
2. He quickly brings one of his powerful Rooks into a good position for either attack or defense.

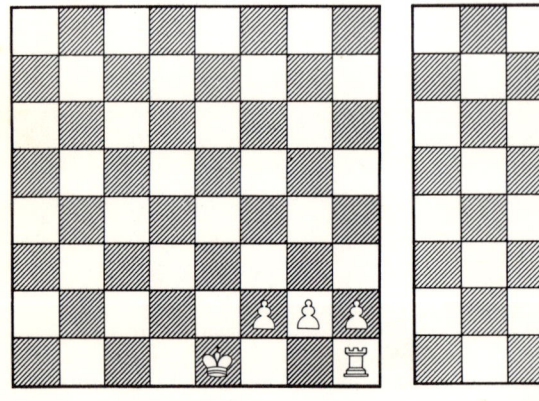

Diagram 40-A 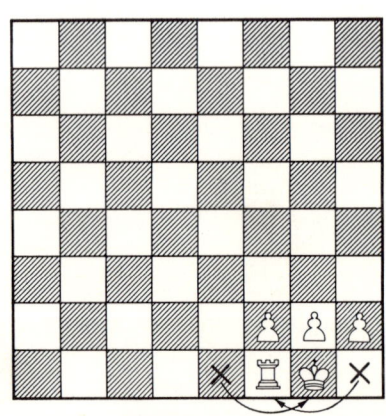   Diagram 40-B

Diagram 40-A shows White about to Castle.

Diagram 40-B shows how the King and the Rook moved, and the position after the Castling move has ended. The King moved two squares over toward the Rook, and the Rook moved to the square which the King skipped over.

Set up your own chessboard as in Diagram 40-A. Pretend you are White and you want to Castle. Say, "I'm Castling"; then make the Castling move yourself.

Although a player moves two pieces when Castling, it counts as one move. Castling is the only time a player may move two of his pieces at once.

You may also Castle on the left side of the board, using the King and the other Rook.

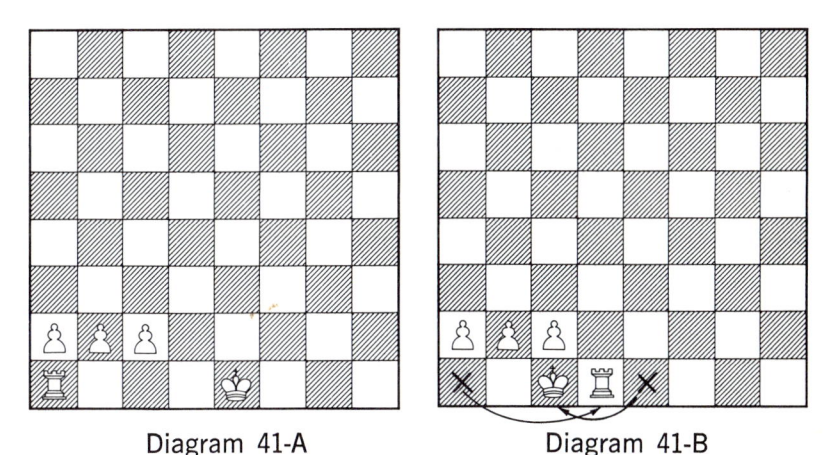

Diagram 41-A   Diagram 41-B

Do the same thing as before: Move the King two squares toward the Rook, and put the Rook on the square which the King skipped over.

RULES FOR CASTLING

A player may Castle only once in a game.

At the time of Castling all of the following five rules must be obeyed:

1. Your King and the Rook used in Castling may not have moved at any time before Castling;

2. All the squares between the King and the Rook must be empty;
3. The King must not be in Check;
4. The King may not move into Check; and
5. The square which the King skips over may not be under attack by any of the opponent's chessmen.

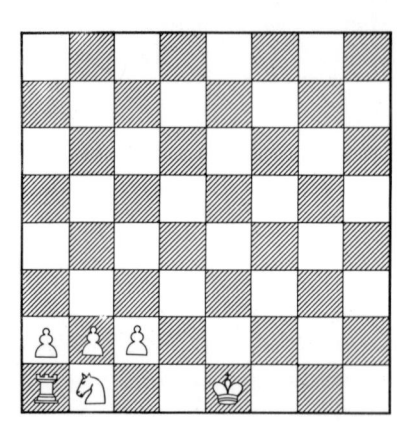

PUZZLES

Diagram 42

Question: Why can't White Castle on the left side of the board?

Answer: There is a Knight on one of the squares between the King and the Rook.

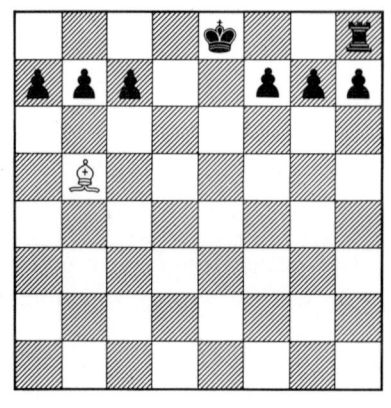

Diagram 43

Question: It's Black's turn to move. Why can't he Castle on this move?

Answer: His King is in Check. He must stop the Check before he will be allowed to Castle.

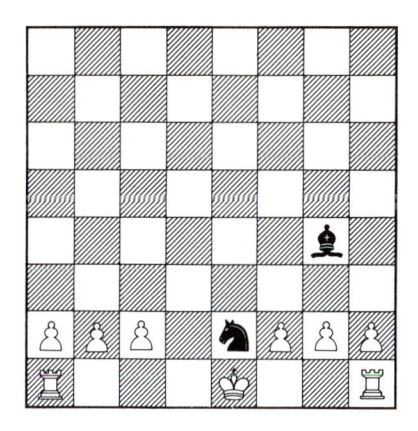

Diagram 44

Question: Can the White King Castle on the left side of the board? Can he Castle on the right side of the board?

Answer: White cannot Castle on either side because if he tried to do so, his King would end up on a square attacked by the Black Knight. Since a King is never allowed to move into Check, White may not Castle as long as the Black Knight remains where he is.

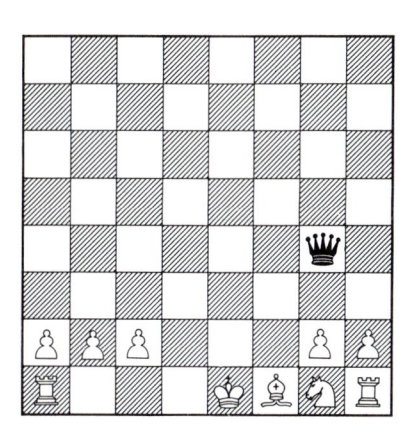

Diagram 45

Question: Why can't White Castle here?

Answer: White's King would have to skip over a square attacked by the Black Queen. So long as the Black Queen attacks that square, White may not Castle on the left side.

Your opponent will usually find it much harder to Checkmate you if you have Castled than he would if you had left your King sitting in the open, just waiting to be attacked from all sides.

In addition, Castling brings your Rooks into action quickly.

Now you know how to move, capture, and Castle. You are ready to play chess! The next chapter will show you how to get started.

CHAPTER 7

Start to Play

The Usual Way to Choose Sides

Behind your back hide a White Pawn in one hand and a Black Pawn in the other. Then bring your closed fists in front of you and let your opponent choose a hand. The color of the Pawn in the hand he chooses will be his color for the first game. (If you play more than one game, you don't choose for each new game; you and your opponent simply change sides each time.)

Setting Up the Chessmen

Let's say your opponent got the Black Pawn. He now sets up his Black chessmen, and you set up your White chessmen, as shown in Diagram 46.

Black

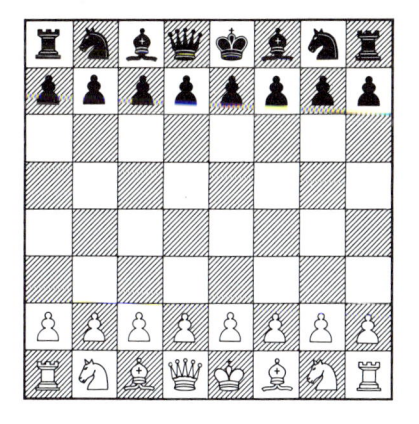

Diagram 46

Remember:
White square
on the right.

White

Notice that each Queen stands on her own color. The White Queen stands on a *white* square, and the Black Queen stands on a *black* square. The Rooks go in the corners, with the Knights next to them.

How to Begin

White always moves first and then Black moves, taking turns. No player may ever take more than one move at a time, and no player may ever skip a turn.

What is a Move?

After you have moved one of your chessmen to some other square on the chessboard and taken your fingers away from that chessman, your move ends. (If you have captured one of your opponent's pieces on that move, you immediately take him off the board, of course.)

The Best Moves to Make

If you are White, make moves toward the center of the board. The center of the board is a good spot from which to launch attacks against the enemy. It's also a good spot from which to defend yourself, in case your opponent tries to attack your King.

1. Start out by moving the Pawn in front of your King two squares forward. (He is called the "King's Pawn.")
2. On your next few moves, bring your Knights and Bishops near the center of the chessboard.
3. Castle fairly early in the game (within the first ten moves or so). This will make it harder for your opponent to threaten your King. It will also allow you to move your Rooks away from the corners and bring them into action when you need them.

If you are Black you, too, should make moves toward the center of the board.

1. If White's first move was to bring his King's Pawn two squares forward, then move your King's Pawn two squares forward also.

    If White's first move was to bring his Queen's Pawn two squares forward, then move your Queen's Pawn two squares forward also.

    If White starts the game by making some other move, then bring either your King's Pawn or Queen's Pawn two squares forward.
2. After your first move, bring your Knights and Bishops out near the center of the board.
3. Castle early.

Notice that whether you are White or Black, the ideas behind these early moves are the same: to try to control the center squares of the board, from which to attack the enemy and defend yourself.

Remember the Purpose of the Game

The whole purpose of the game is to Checkmate your opponent's King, and to prevent him from Checkmating you. Keep looking for ways to Checkmate him all through the game.

Capture Your Opponent's Pieces

Try to find ways to capture your opponent's pieces outright or to make winning exchanges.

Threaten Your Opponent's Pieces

Move so that you threaten to capture an enemy piece on your next turn. Most of all, attack his more powerful pieces with your smaller ones whenever you can. Write down the values of the pieces on a sheet of paper, (see page 22), and keep the copy next to the chessboard as you play. This will help you remember which pieces are the most important.

Protect Your Own Pieces

If your opponent is threatening to capture one of your Pawns, for example, protect that Pawn with one of your other pieces. (That is, move your other piece into such position so that if he captures your Pawn you'll be able to capture his piece in exchange.) Even if your opponent is not threatening to make a capture, it's still a good idea to position your pieces so that they protect one another.

Attack With Force

Most successful attacks are made by aiming a number of pieces at one spot.

Sometimes you may be able to move just one piece into enemy territory and do some damage. But since your opponent will be defending himself, you'll more often have to attack with two or three or more of your men working together.

Play as many games as you can, with as many different people as possible; and in order to improve your play, continue reading this book in between your games.

PLAYING TO WIN

CHAPTER 8

Names and Abbreviations

Chess "notation" is a kind of code which makes it possible to describe each chess move in a simple and short way. For example, instead of saying "The Bishop on the King's side of the board moved to the fifth square in front of the Knight on the Queen's side," we can say "KB-QN5."

This method of notation is very easy to learn.

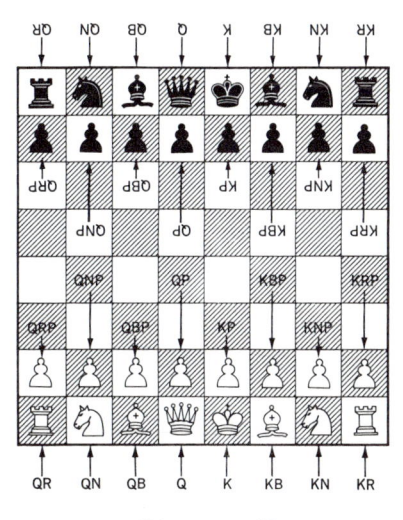

Diagram 47

Diagram 47 shows how the board is set up at the start of every game. The letters in the diagram are abbreviations for the exact names of the chessmen in their starting lineup.

Diagram 48 lists the exact name of every chessman at the start of a game, together with the abbreviation for its name:

Queen's Rook Pawn	Queen's Knight Pawn	Queen's Bishop Pawn	Queen's Pawn	King's Pawn	King's Bishop Pawn	King's Knight Pawn	King's Rook Pawn
QRP	QNP	QBP	QP	KP	KBP	KNP	KRP
Queen's Rook	Queen's Knight	Queen's Bishop	Queen	King	King's Bishop	King's Knight	King's Rook
QR	QN	QB	Q	K	KB	KN	KR

Diagram 48

The abbreviations are just the first letters of the words, except for the letter N, which stands for the word Knight. The reason N is used for Knight is that the letter K already stands for King.

Names and Abbreviations of the Squares

The squares of the chessboard get their names from the original position of the pieces. For example, the square on which the King stands at the start of a game (in the first row or 1st Rank) is called "King 1." The square in front of the King (in the 2nd Rank) is called "King 2." The square in front of that (in the 3rd Rank) is called "King 3," and so on. The names of the squares are abbreviated, to K1, K2, K3, etc.

Diagram 49 shows the abbreviation for the name of each square. You'll see that actually each square has two "names," one for the White player and one for the Black player.

1st Rank	QR1 / QR8	QN1 / QN8	QB1 / QB8	Q1 / Q8	K1 / K8	KB1 / KB8	KN1 / KN8	KR1 / KR8	8th Rank
2nd Rank	QR2 / QR7	QN2 / QN7	QB2 / QB7	Q2 / Q7	K2 / K7	KB2 / KB7	KN2 / KN7	KR2 / KR7	7th Rank
3rd Rank	QR3 / QR6	QN3 / QN6	QB3 / QB6	Q3 / Q6	K3 / K6	KB3 / KB6	KN3 / KN6	KR3 / KR6	6th Rank
4th Rank	QR4 / QR5	QN4 / QN5	QB4 / QB5	Q4 / Q5	K4 / K5	KB4 / KB5	KN4 / KN5	KR4 / KR5	5th Rank
5th Rank	QR5 / QR4	QN5 / QN4	QB5 / QB4	Q5 / Q4	K5 / K4	KB5 / KB4	KN5 / KN4	KR5 / KR4	4th Rank
6th Rank	QR6 / QR3	QN6 / QN3	QB6 / QB3	Q6 / Q3	K6 / K3	KB6 / KB3	KN6 / KN3	KR6 / KR3	3rd Rank
7th Rank	QR7 / QR2	QN7 / QN2	QB7 / QB2	Q7 / Q2	K7 / K2	KB7 / KB2	KN7 / KN2	KR7 / KR2	2nd Rank
8th Rank	QR8 / QR1	QN8 / QN1	QB8 / QB1	Q8 / Q1	K8 / K1	KB8 / KB1	KN8 / KN1	KR8 / KR1	1st Rank

Black   White

Diagram 49

If you think it will be hard for you to remember the names of the squares, put this book on the table next to your chessboard, and keep it open to Diagram 49 as you play. In that way you'll get to know the names of the squares easily.

CHAPTER 9

The Opening

"The Opening" is the beginning stage of a chess game. It's the time during which each player moves many of his pieces away from their original squares, usually toward the center of the board. It's the period during which each player gets ready to make strong attacks and also gets set to defend himself.

The Opening is very important, for a good beginning will help you to win the game. Let's look at the first few moves of a game in which both White and Black make good opening moves.

Play out each of these moves on your own chessboard so you can see what's happening. (Use Diagram 49 to help you.)

White	Black	
1 KP-K4		(White's first move: King's Pawn to square K4) This is an excellent move. White immediately has a Pawn in the center of the board, and at the same time has opened up a diagonal in case his King's Bishop wants to move out quickly.

White	Black
1	KP-K4

(Black's first move: King's Pawn to square K4) A good answer by Black. Not only does this move give him a Pawn in the center of the board, but it also blocks White's KP from moving any farther ahead.

2 KN-KB3

(King's Knight to square KB3)
White threatens Black's KP immediately with this move. Even if Black defends his Pawn on the next move, White's Knight is in a good jumping-off spot for other attacks later in the game.

2 .... QN-QB3

(Queen's Knight to square QB3)
Black moves one of his Knights out toward the center of the board also, and at the same time defends his KP. If White's Knight were now to capture Black's Pawn (a value of 1), Black's Knight would take the White Knight (a value of 3).

3 KB-QB4

(King's Bishop to square QB4)

Diagram 50, below, shows the position after White's third move. Check your own board to see that it looks like this:

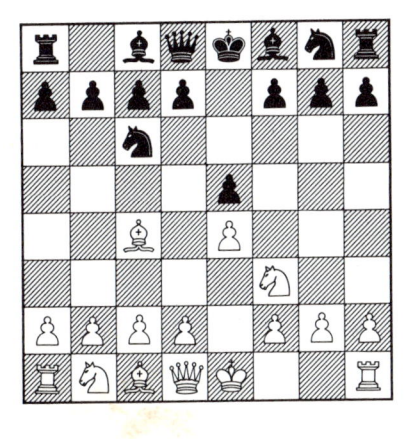

Diagram 50

White	Black

With his third move White does three things:
1. He clears the spaces between his King and his King's Rook, so that he's ready to Castle anytime he wants;
2. His Bishop is out near the center of the board, which is often a good place for him;
3. His Bishop is attacking the Black Pawn at Black's square KB2. (Each player's square KB2 is the weakest point at the beginning of a game.) White won't capture Black's KBP on his next move because the Black King would capture the Bishop in return. However, it's always good to threaten as much as possible. (After only three moves, White is threatening two things: his Knight is attacking Black's KP, and his Bishop is attacking Black's KBP.)

3......... KB-QB4   (King's Bishop to square QB4)
Black threatens White's square KB2 and also clears one of the spaces between his King and his King's Rook.

4 QP-Q3   (Queen's Pawn to square Q3)
The QP now defends both the KP and the KB against future attack. This move also opens up the diagonal so the QB can come out.

4......... KN-KB3   (King's Knight to square KB3)
With this move the spaces between Black's K and his KR are cleared, so he may Castle on his next move, if he wishes. Black's KN is in a good position near the center of the board, and is also threatening White's KP. In this position,

White	Black

Black's KN won't capture White's KP (a value of 1) because then White's QP would capture the KN (a value of 3). Yet, it's not a bad idea to threaten the opponent's men whenever possible.

5 QB-KN5   (Queen's Bishop to square KN5)

Diagram 51 shows the position after White's fifth move:

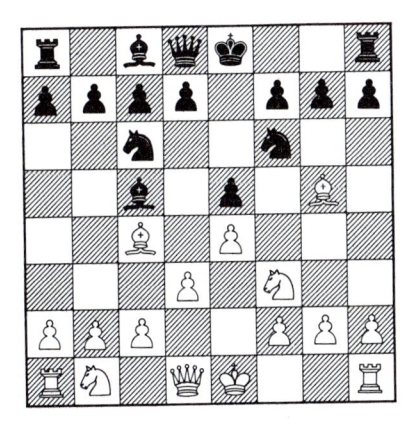

Diagram 51

White's QB is now in a position to capture Black's KN (a value of 3); but if he did so, Black's Q would then simply take White's QB (a value of 3.) This would be an even exchange, and White wouldn't have gained anything.

The real reason for the QB's move to KN5 is to "freeze" or "pin" the Knight. As long as the Bishop stays where he is, Black's KN doesn't dare move away. (If the Knight did move, White's QB would then capture his opponent's Queen (a value of 9)—a terrible loss of power for Black.)

White	Black
5......... QP-Q3	

(Queen's Pawn to square Q3)
Black's QP now protects his KP and his KB; and the diagonal is opened for Black's QB to move out.

6 0-0

(White Castles on the King's side)
By Castling, White's King is now safer behind friendly Pawns, and his Rook is in a better position to move into action.

6............. 0-0

(Black Castles on the King's side)
Black Castles for the same reason that White did.

Note: The notation 0-0 means the player has Castled on the King's side. The two zeros stand for the two empty squares between the King and the King's Rook.

The notation 0-0-0 would mean the player has Castled on the Queen's side. The three zeros stand for the three empty squares between the King and the Queen's Rook.

7 QN-QB3

(Queen's Knight to square QB3)
White brings additional power out toward the center of the board.

7.......... QB-K3

(Queen's Bishop to square K3)
Black doesn't mind if White's Bishop captures the Black QB (a value of 3), because then Black's KBP would take White's Bishop (a value of 3). This would be an even exchange, but it would take some pressure off Black and allow his pieces more room to set up a possible attack against the White King.

This is how the chessboard would look after Black's seventh move:

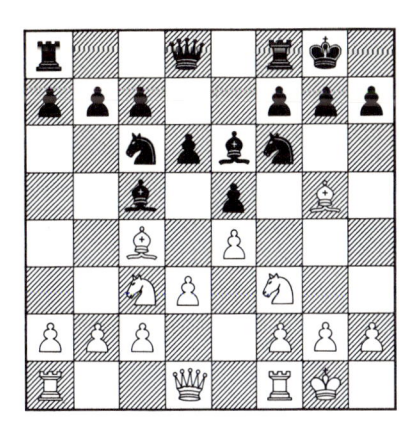

Diagram 52

Each player has a solid position. Notice that each player has moved his pieces toward the center of the board.

Using the example of a good opening given on the preceding pages, here are some suggestions for you to follow in the early stages of each of your games:

1. Moves toward the center of the board are usually good.

Pawns. At the start of a game, moving your KP or QP (or sometimes one of your Bishops' Pawns) is much better than moving the Knights' Pawns or the Rooks' Pawns. Your opponent will be trying to mass his pieces in the center, from which to launch a powerful attack against you. By making early moves with your center Pawns you'll be throwing up roadblocks against him. In addition, these early moves by your KP and QP open up the diagonals, so that you can bring out your Bishops and possibly set up an attack of your own.

Knights and *Bishops:* After one or two Pawn moves, develop your Knights and Bishops. (In chess, to "develop" a piece means to move it from its original square and onto a square which is better for attack and defense. Usually the best squares for the Knights' first moves are KB3 and QB3. Two good squares for the Bishops are KB4 and QB4.

2. Bring out new pieces rather than move the same piece a second or third time.

In other words, in the early stages of the game move a piece to a good square. If he's not attacked, leave him there while you bring out some other pieces. It's usually good to develop as many different pieces as possible so that a number of your men will be able to work together when you make a drive to smash the enemy defenses.

The best squares for most of your chessmen are *not* their original squares. You'll have a better chance to win the game if you develop most of your pieces swiftly—except for the Queen. In general, it's not a good idea to bring out the Queen immediately. The reason for this is that if your opponent plays properly he'll threaten her with his smaller pieces. As a result, while your Queen is being chased around looking for a safe spot, your opponent will be rapidly developing his Knights and Bishops. (Usually it's best to wait until after you've Castled before bringing out the Queen.)

3. Castle early (within the first 10 moves or so).

As long as your King sits on his original square, he's subject to attack from many directions. Castling carries him to a safer home behind friendly Pawns.

Castling also permits you to bring your powerful Rooks into position to support your other pieces in the center of the board.

CHAPTER 10

Early Queen Attacks

Although it's generally not wise for a player to bring out his Queen too early, some players still do it. In this chapter we'll look into the moves that should and should not be made in answer to an early Queen attack.

First let's look at an early Queen attack by White which succeeds after only four moves because Black did not defend himself properly. This series of moves is so well known that it has a name of its own: Scholar's Mate.

Set up your board as in Diagram 46, and then make each of the moves yourself so you can see what's going on.

55

White	Black	
1 KP-K4	KP-K4	Each side makes a good first move.
2 Q-R5		White's Queen threatens to Check the Black King by capturing his KP. The Q also threatens the Pawn on Black's square KB2.
2	.QN-QB3	Black develops his QN and protects his KP. This is a good move.
3 KB-QB4		White's KB threatens Black's Pawn on square KB2. Now White's Bishop and Queen are both attacking that square.
3	.KN-KB3	Black develops his KN, which ordinarily is a fine move—but in this case it's disaster because he just hasn't looked carefully enough at White's last two moves.
4 QxBP mate		(*x* means *captures;* *mate* means *Checkmate.*) White's Queen captures the Pawn at Black's square KB2. The Black King is in Check and cannot get out of Check. The game is over!

Diagram 53

Diagram 53 shows the final position of "Scholar's Mate." Many beginners have lost their first games of chess in just this way.

In view of the way the Scholar's Mate game ended, you may wonder why it was suggested in the last chapter that you *not* bring out your Queen immediately. The game which follows shows the reason: If a player moves correctly he will not only beat back such an early attack by the Queen, but he'll also end up in a better position.

Set up your board as in Diagram 46 and make each of the following moves yourself.

White	Black
1 KP-K4	KP-K4
2 Q-R5	QN-QB3

3 KB-QB4   Up to this point the moves are the same as in Scholar's Mate. But watch the move that Black makes now!

3....... KNP-KN3   Black has seen that White threatens Checkmate at square KB2. By moving his KNP to KN3 he stops the Mate—and the KNP is now attacking the White Queen! (If the White Q takes the attacking Pawn, she'll be captured herself.)

4 Q-KB3   White moves his Q to square KB3. He again threatens Checkmate at Black's square KB2.

4.........KN-KB3   Black's KN at KB3 blocks the White Q from attacking square KB2. (If White's Q were to capture the KN, The Black Q would take the White Q.)

5 QP-Q3   White's main reason for making this move is to open up the diagonal. He wants to move his QB to KN5 so that his QB and his Q would both be attacking Black's KN.

5..........QN-Q5!   (*An exclamation mark indicates a very good move.*)
Black won't give White a chance to carry out his plans; he launches an attack of

White	Black
	his own! In moving his QN to Q5 Black sets up two serious threats: (1) He is attacking White's Q; (2) He threatens to capture White's QBP and Check the King (then after the K moved out of Check, the Black Knight would capture White's QR).
6 Q-Q1	After all that running around, White's Q has to go back to its original square! (It's the only way White can get his Q out of danger and also protect his square QB2 against the Black Knight's attack.)
6	KB-KN2

Diagram 54 shows the position at the end of Black's sixth move.

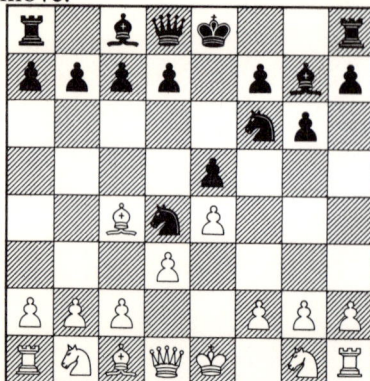

Diagram 54

After only six moves, Black has successfully defended himself. He is ready to Castle, and he has developed two Knights and a Bishop while White has developed only one Bishop. The game isn't over, but Black is in fine shape.

Don't be afraid of early Queen attacks by your opponent. Be careful to protect yourself, of course, but look upon it as a good chance to chase his Queen away with your smaller pieces and to set up a strong counterattack of your own.

Is there *ever* a time when you should move your Queen out

early? Yes. If your opponent plays badly and offers you a golden opportunity, take advantage of it! In the game which follows, White plays badly. This is the quickest Checkmate possible in chess.

Play out the moves on your own board.

White	Black
1 KBP-KB3?	(*A question mark is used to show a bad move.*)
1 .... KP-K4	A good first move by Black.
2 KNP-KN4??	(*Two question marks indicate a terrible move.*)
2 ...... Q-R5 mate!	Black had planned to bring out his center Pawns and then to develop his Knights and Bishops. But when he saw the second bad move by White, he immediately made the most of the opportunity.

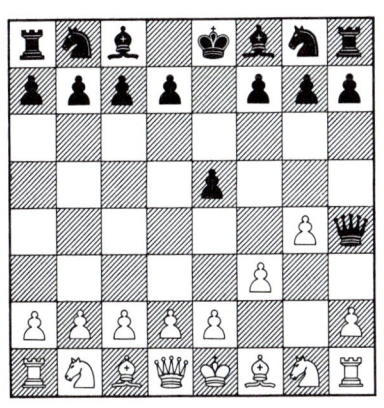

Diagram 55

As you can see from this disastrously short game, it's not safe to move your KBP and KNP early unless you have a certain plan in mind and know exactly what you're doing. If your opponent makes these weak moves, see if you can find a way either to Checkmate him or otherwise attack him seriously.

There may be other occasions when you think it wise to move your Queen out immediately. You may be right. Just keep in mind that she is extremely valuable. Move her with care.

CHAPTER 11

When and How to Attack

As you play, always look for a chance to Checkmate your opponent's King—for if you can do that you won't have to worry about doing anything else.

At first, the enemy King will be so well protected that you'll have no way of attacking him directly. To weaken his defenses, you'll want to attack and capture as many enemy pieces as you can, so keep looking for signs that an attack might be worth while. Here are some of those signs:

An Unprotected Piece

If you notice that one of your opponent's pieces is not protected by any of his other chessmen, see if you can find a safe way to attack it.

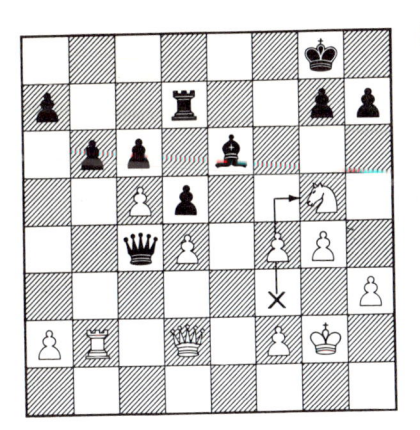

Diagram 56

Diagram 56: White has just moved his Knight from square KB3 to square KN5, attacking Black's Bishop. If Black doesn't want to lose his Bishop outright he'll have to either retreat or bring up another piece to defend it.

A Weakly Defended Piece

If one of your opponent's pieces is protected by only one of his other men, try to attack that piece with two of your men.

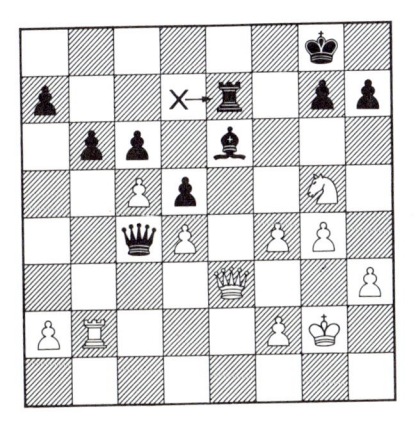

Diagram 57-A

Diagram 57-A is the same as 56, except that Black has moved his Rook to his square K2, defending the Bishop. Now if White's Knight were to capture the Black Bishop (a value of 3), Black's Rook would take the White Knight (a value of 3). This would

61

be an even exchange. (Knights and Bishops have about the same value.)

Instead of making the even exchange, White now decides to attack Black's Bishop with a second piece, this time his Queen, as shown in the next diagram.

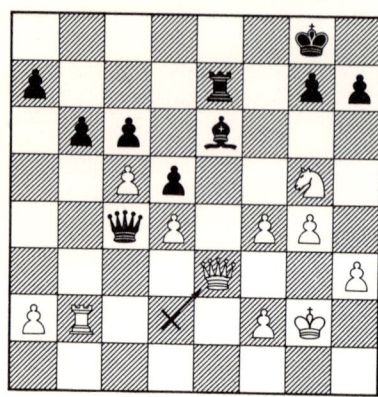

Diagram 57-B

As Diagram 57-B shows, Black must now move his Bishop away in order to save it. (Black has had to use up his turns in defending himself and running away, while White is free to set up some more threats.)

If Black made some other move and did not retreat his Bishop, here is what might happen:

    White   Black
1 NxB   RxN
2 QxR

(Remember, "x" means "captures")

White would capture a Bishop and Rook (a total value of 8), and Black would capture only a Knight (a value of 3). This would be a very good exchange for White.

Note that White, in this case, must not make the first capture with his Queen. If he did, he would lose the exchange!

    White   Black
1 QxB   RxQ
2 NxR

White would capture a Bishop and Rook (a total value of 8), but he would lose his Queen (worth 9).

When you're attacking one of your opponent's men with two or more of your own, it is often good to make the first capture with the smallest of your attacking pieces.

A Piece Stuck in a Bad Spot

If you see one of your opponent's pieces stuck in a spot where he doesn't have too much room to move around, try to trap the piece.

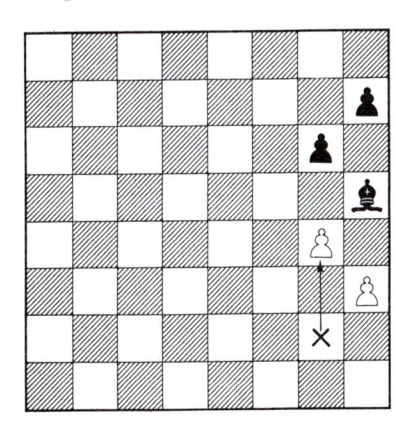

Diagram 58

White has just moved his Pawn from KN2 to KN4. Black's Bishop is now trapped, and all he can get in exchange for it is a White Pawn.

In each of your games there will be many opportunities to threaten your opponent's bigger pieces with your smaller ones. (Diagram 58 is an example). Threaten your opponent's bigger pieces as often as you can, for even if he runs away, you may spoil his plans and get him into trouble.

CHAPTER 12

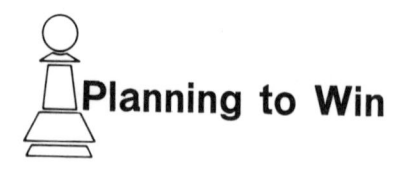

Planning to Win

A Plan of Action

Remember that your goals are to Checkmate your opponent's King while protecting your own.

Develop Your Pieces Early

1. Move out your KP and/or QP as soon as possible.
2. Quickly develop your Knights and Bishops to good squares toward the center of the board.
3. Castle early.

Attack

1. Try to capture your opponent's pieces so that you get ahead in power.

2. If you can capture a piece by using only one of your men, then do it; usually, your opponent will defend himself, though, so try to attack one of his pieces with several of yours.

When to Exchange

1. Make winning exchanges as often as possible.
2. When you are already ahead in power, make winning exchanges or even exchanges.
3. When your pieces are cramped or a position is very complicated and confusing, you may loosen things up by making winning exchanges or even exchanges.

Rooks and Queen

1. After Castling, move your Rooks and Queen into the action. Use them to support your other pieces and to launch strong attacks against the enemy.

Figure Out What Your Opponent Is Planning

1. Ask yourself why your opponent moved as he did.
   After he moves you may want to change your plans.
2. If his last move was weak, see if you can take advantage of it by Mating him immediately, or capturing one of his big pieces, or getting a better position than you expected.
3. If his last move was strong, you may have to concentrate on defending yourself, or you may have to bring more pieces into play against him, or you may have to move your attack to one of his weaker spots.

CHAPTER **13**

More Openings

Some opening moves have become so well known that they've been given names.

This chapter introduces you to a few openings which are relatively simple and yet often lead to very exciting games. Each of these openings emphasizes swift development and early control of the center of the board, with the idea of quickly attacking the enemy King.

Play each of these openings out on your own board, and then experiment with further moves which White or Black might make.

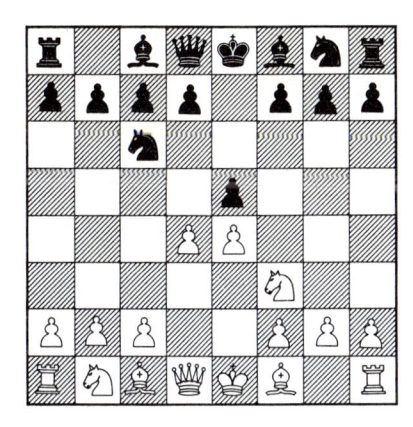

Diagram 59

The Scotch Game

WHITE	BLACK
1 KP-K4	KP-K4
2 KN-KB3	QN-QB3
3 QP-Q4	

If Black then plays 3........PxQP, White would play 4 NxP. If Black continues with 4........NxN, then White could play 5 QxN.

On your own board continue White's development and see what attacking possibilities he might have.

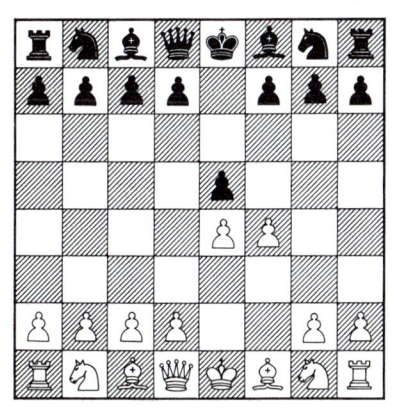

Diagram 60

The King's Gambit ("Gambit" means "sacrifice"; that is, purposely losing a Pawn so as to get a strong attacking position.)

WHITE	BLACK
1 KP-K4	KP-K4
2 KBP-KB4	

Black then usually plays 2........PxBP. White's third move is KN-KB3—not only to develop his King's Knight, but also to stop Black's Queen from moving to Black's square KR5, from which point the Queen could do a lot of damage.

After White makes his third move, his idea will be to develop both Bishops, and Castle on the King's side.

The King's Gambit almost always leads to a wide-open game, with great attacking possibilities for White if Black doesn't defend carefully.

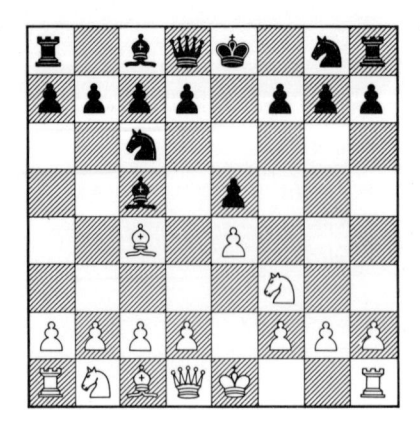

Diagram 61

The Giuoco Piano

WHITE	BLACK
1 KP-K4	KP-K4
2 KN-KB3	QN-QB3
3 KB QB4	KB-QB4

In Chapter 9 you saw one example of how the Giuoco Piano might be played.

On your own chessboard, play out the first three moves listed above, and then experiment with various further moves by both Black and White. (One of White's purposes in this opening is to put pressure on Black's KBP.)

Play the Scotch Game, the King's Gambit, and the Giuoco Piano as often as you can, so that you become very familiar with them.
On the other hand, don't be afraid to experiment with other kinds of openings or some other ideas of your own. You may very well learn something which could be of great value to you in later games.

ADVANCED RULES AND SUGGESTIONS

CHAPTER **14**

More on Check

Discovered Check

Discovered Check is really just like any other Check, except that it is a way of taking your opponent by surprise.

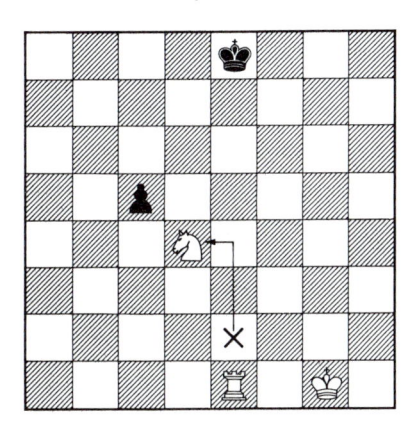

Diagram 62

Diagram 62 shows that White's Knight has just moved from K2 to Q4. After White made the move, he said "Check!" Black was surprised. How could the White Knight Check the King

71

from so far away? Then Black looked back to where the Knight had come from and discovered that it was the White Rook which Checked the King. The White Rook had been hiding behind his Knight, ready to Check the Black King as soon as the Knight moved away. (As you can see from this example, you don't have to Check with the piece you are moving.)

Notice also in Diagram 62 that although Black's Pawn is in a position to capture the White Knight, he won't be allowed to do it on this move because he must first get his King out of Check.

The next two diagrams show some more examples of Discovered Check. In each case it is White's turn to move.

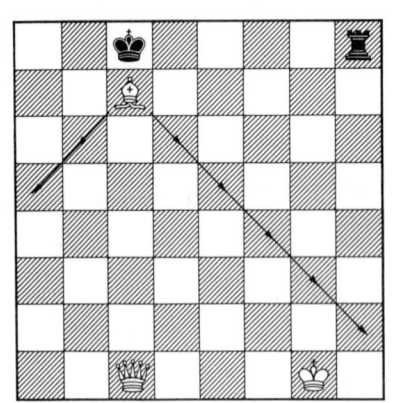

Diagram 63-A

Diagram 63-A: White's Bishop can move to a number of squares, leaving his Queen to Check the Black King.

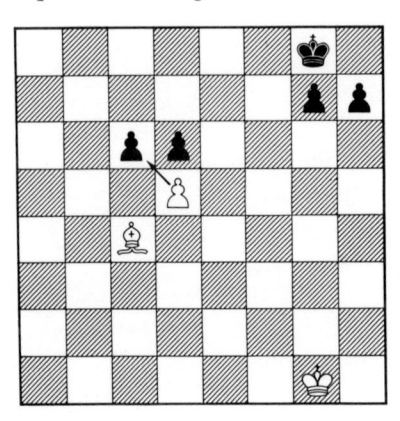

Diagram 63-B

Diagram 63-B: If White can get his own Pawn out of the way, his Bishop could Check the Black King. White's Pawn cannot move straight forward because a Black Pawn is blocking his way. However, he can move out of the way by capturing the other Black Pawn.

Double Check

Double Check means that in one move a player Checks his opponent's King with two different pieces. Double Checks don't happen too often in chess games; but when they do, they can be very powerful moves.

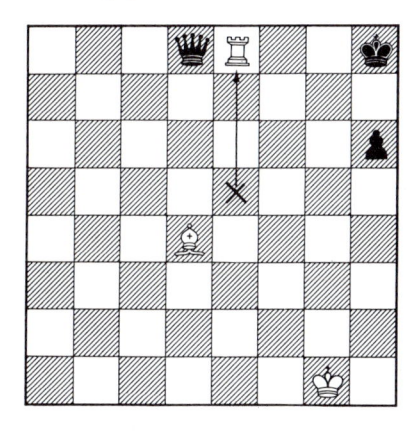

Diagram 64

Diagram 64 shows that White's Rook has just moved from K5 to K8.

Black's King is attacked twice: by the Rook (a regular Check), and by the Bishop (a Discovered Check). Black's Queen would like to capture the White Rook but is not allowed to, since that would not stop the Check on the Black King by the Bishop.

So the only thing Black can do to get out of *both* Checks is to move his King to a safe square.

(The Double Check was an excellent move by White because after the Black King moves to a safe square White's Rook can capture the Black Queen!)

CHAPTER **15**

En Passant

Now we come to a special capturing move that can only be made by a Pawn on an enemy Pawn's first move. This is called "capturing *en passant*." *En passant* is a French term which means "in passing" or "as it passes by."

If you spend just a short time going over the next few pages, you won't have much trouble learning what this special capturing move is all about.

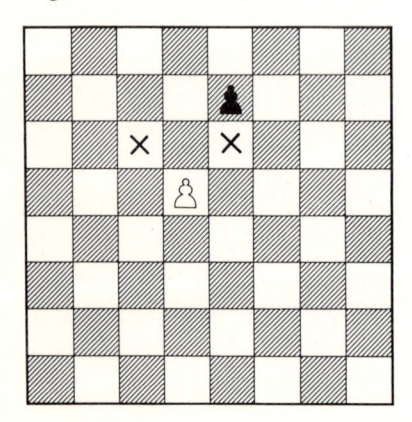

Diagram 65

Look at Diagram 65. The two squares attacked by the White Pawn are marked with an x.

In Diagram 65, the Black Pawn is about to make *its first move;* so, as you learned earlier, it may go one square forward or two squares forward, as it chooses.

If the Black Pawn moved only one square forward, it would be in a square marked with an x. The White Pawn could then capture the Black Pawn in the usual way, if he wanted to.

But let's say that instead of moving one square forward the Black Pawn decides to go *two* squares forward on its first move, "passing by" the square attacked by the White Pawn.

Now, on White's turn to move, what may *he* do?

If he wishes to, he may capture Black's Pawn *en passant* (as it passes by). In other words, White may now capture Black's Pawn because the Black Pawn "passed by" a square which White's Pawn was attacking.

(White doesn't *have* to capture Black's Pawn *en passant,* but if he chooses to do so, he must do it right away, on his very next move.)

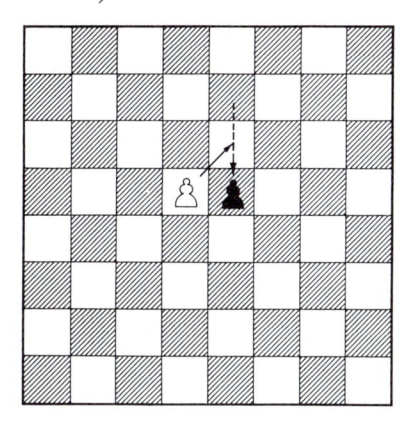

Diagram 66

Look at Diagram 66. After Black's Pawn moves two squares forward, White's Pawn captures *en passant* by moving into the square which the Black Pawn passed over. Black's Pawn is removed from the board, of course, because he has been captured.

CHAPTER 16

Draws

A Draw is a tie game; neither player wins and neither player loses.

There are six different ways to Draw in Chess:

1. Not Enough Material When neither side has enough power left to Checkmate the other, the game is a Draw. For example:

A King alone can never Checkmate the other King.

A King and a Knight alone are not enough power to Checkmate the other King.

A King and a Bishop alone are not enough power to Checkmate the other King.

2. Stalemate   A Stalemate occurs when a player cannot make any legal move, although it is his turn to move, and his King is *not* in Check.

Often a King and a Pawn can win against a lone King (if the Pawn can reach its 8th Rank and turn into a Queen). But sometimes a lone King can get a Stalemate against a King and a Pawn. Such a Stalemate is shown in Diagram 67.

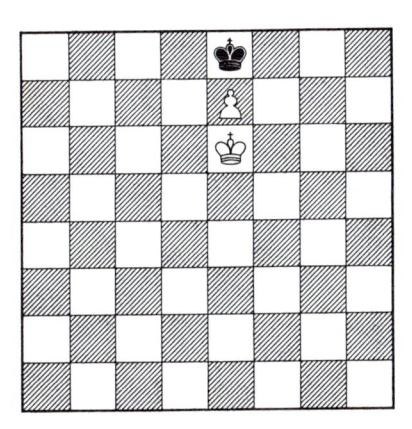

Diagram 67

This is a Stalemate. It is Black's turn to move, but any move he could make would put his King in Check. (He cannot capture the White Pawn because it is protected by its own King. He also cannot move into either of the white squares, because these squares are attacked by White's King. He cannot move into either of the black squares, because these two squares are attacked by White's Pawn.)

Black is supposed to move, but he has no other pieces left in the game, and he is not allowed to move his King. Since Black cannot make any legal move, but his King *is not in Check*, it's not Checkmate—it's Stalemate, or a Draw. If in one of your games you have many more pieces left than your opponent, and you think you should win easily, be careful that he doesn't get a Stalemate instead of losing to you.

3. Perpetual Check   Perpetual Check occurs when a player can Check his opponent's King forever, but cannot actually Checkmate him.

Diagram 68 shows a position where Black gains a Draw by Perpetual Check even though he's far behind in power. His Queen has just Checked the White King.

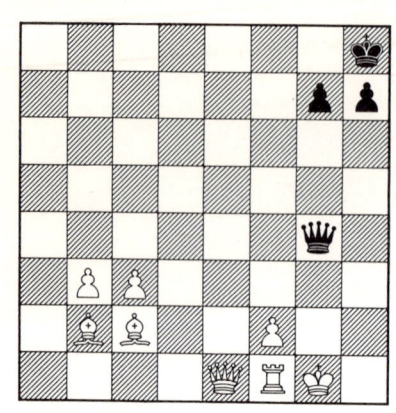

Diagram 68

White must get out of Check, and the only way he can do that is by moving his King to square KR1 or square KR2. But then Black moves his Queen to *his* square KR5 and Checks the White King again.

As long as Black keeps moving his Queen back and forth between his squares KR5 and KN5 he can keep Checking the White King forever. The game ends in a Draw.

4. By Agreement When both players agree to call the game a Draw, the game ends at that point as a Draw.

Don't ever let yourself be "talked into" a Draw by your opponent. The only time you should agree to a Draw is when you *want* to agree to it.

5. 50-Move Rule When no capture is made by either side and no Pawn is moved by either side for 50 moves in a row by each player, it's a Draw.

This is very unusual, and you probably won't have reason to use this rule.

6. Exact Position Repeated Three Times When the *exact* position of *all* the pieces on both sides is repeated three times (and it's the same player's turn to move after the third time as it was before the first time) then it is a Draw.

This rule, too, will come up very rarely in your games. It was included in the list only so you'd know that such a rule exists.

CHAPTER 17

Touch-Move

Touch-Move is a rule that tournament players *must* use, and one that you should follow in every game you play.

First, if it's your turn to move and you touch one of your pieces, you *must move it*.

However, this does not apply in the following cases:

1. If moving the piece you touched would put your King into Check.

2. If, while your King is in Check, moving the touched piece would not get your King out of Check.

3. If the chessman you touched simply cannot make a move.

Second, if it's your turn to move and you touch one of your opponent's pieces, you *must capture it,* if at all possible.

However, this does not apply in the following cases:

1. If only one of your chessmen can capture the touched opponent's piece, and moving that one particular chessman of yours would put your King into Check.

2. If, while your King is in Check, capturing the touched opponent's piece would not get your King out of Check.

3. If none of your men can actually capture the touched opponent's piece.

A Helpful Hint

Don't rush to touch a piece. For instance, suppose your opponent has just moved and said "Check." Don't panic. Don't grab your King right away and then try to figure out your best move. Or, let's say your opponent has just moved his Queen and you see that you can capture it with one of your Knights. Don't snap up the bait too quickly! First make sure no hook is attached to the bait. Your opponent may *want* you to take his Queen, so that he can Checkmate you on his next move with one of his other pieces!

Always look the situation over carefully *before* you touch any of your pieces or any of your opponent's pieces.

If you make yourself follow this Touch-Move rule game after game, you'll slowly learn two things deep down inside your mind:

1. You'll learn to make fewer hasty moves and fewer bad moves.

2. You'll learn to get in the habit of thinking ahead.

Whether your opponent plays Touch-Move or not, make sure you do. It's the only way to become a good chess player.

Be fair about these rules with your opponent. If he's also playing Touch-Move and accidentally touches his Queen, say, while he's reaching for a banana or a baloney sandwich, don't insist that he has to move his Queen because he touched it.

How a Move Ends

When you lift your fingers off a piece, after moving it to another square, your move has ended. However, until the time you take your hand away from the piece you may change your mind as to where you want to put it.

J'adoube

Sometimes, for one reason or another, one of the chessmen may not be exactly in the center of a square. If you want to rearrange it you must tell your opponent you're only centering the piece *before you touch it*. Tournament players do this by saying *"J'adoube"* which is a French term meaning "I adjust."

CHAPTER **18**

Final Thoughts

How to Make a Record of Your Games

(1) Write down the abbreviation for the name of the chessman which has just moved.

(2) Then write down the abbreviation for the name of the square to which that chessman has moved. (Remember that when you are recording White's move you must give the name of the square from *his* point of view; and when it is Black who has just moved you must give the name of the square from *Black's* point of view. Use Diagram 49, on page 47, to help you.)

Be sure to include your name and the name of your opponent, so that when you review the game a few weeks later you'll know who played this particular game and which of you was White and which one Black. Also make sure you record each move in the correct column.

Here is a short example of the beginning of a game:

WHITE (Name of person)	BLACK (Name of person)	DATE
1 P-K4	P-K4	
2 N-KB3	N-QB3	
3 P-Q4	PxP	
4 NxP	NxN	
5 QxN	........and so on	

Sometimes it's not necessary to give the chessman's full abbreviation. For instance, *P-K4* means the KP has moved to square K4. The reason we don't have to write *KP-K4* is that no Pawn other than the KP can go to square K4 at this point in the game. However, it's never wrong to put down the full abbreviation or any other information you might want to record. Just be certain it's clear which piece moved where.

After you've recorded a number of games you might want to play some of them over again, all by yourself, either for fun or to see where you might have made better moves.

If there is any question you have about playing chess, write to the author in care of the publisher. (You must enclose a self-addressed stamped envelope with your letter.)

Now play chess—the greatest game in the world!